What people are saying about
The Tao of Motherhood...

"Vimala McClure, author of the classic *Infant Massage: A Handbook for Loving Parents*, gives us yet another loving guide. It is a book to pick up, draw a deep breath from, and rely upon for reading some calm and sense into your day."

—Joan Logghe, **Mothering Magazine**

"McClure has produced a very fine piece of work... The root theme is conscious mothering. Within this theme is a wealth of insight into the inner child and the greater outer child—which is society. This is a wonderful book which in itself is a demonstration of how mothering (nurturing) can be expanded beyond the parenting of biological children. *The Tao of Motherhood* is very wise, soothing and beautiful."

—Joseph A. Terrano, **Friend's Review**

"A gentle and harmonious collection of meditations."

—**Creation Spirituality**

"*The Tao of Motherhood* is perfect bedside reading for a weary mother... Its passages are brief, poetic and inspiring. In a society that can't quite acknowledge the value of good parenting or the difficulties inherent in doing the job well, succinct guidance and support are nice to find."

—Abigail Lewis, **Whole Life Times**

"I am a single father, finding myself sometimes at a loss with my daughter as to how to nurture her with the love and understanding that I often associate with the mothers of this world... *The Tao of Motherhood* is like a Rosetta stone. I found myself more available and gentle and nurturing, not only to my seven-year-old daughter but also to myself. Thank you!"

—Greg Pavlich, Boulder, Colorado

"*The Tao of Motherhood* is a beautiful testament of motherhood. It is always close at hand and I thank you for helping to keep me on my spiritual journey."

—A. Smith, Ottowa, Ontario

"I read parts of *The Tao of Motherhood* daily for inspiration. The words speak to me with such clarity, and give me much to strive for in my relationship with my two daughters. Many thanks for this book—it is a source of joy to me."

—Susan Shepard, Boulder, Colorado

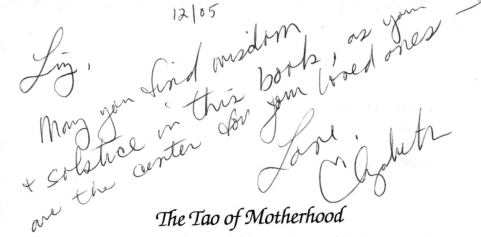

12/05

Liz,

May you find wisdom
& solstice in this book, as you
are the center for your loved ones —

Love,
Elizabeth

The Tao of Motherhood

by Vimala McClure

NUCLEUS Publications
"Books for Personal, Family
and Community Well-Being"

The Tao of Motherhood
Vimala McClure

Illustrated by Michael B. McClure

Published by NUCLEUS Publications, Rt 2, Box 49,
Willow Springs, MO 65793. **Send for free catalog.**

Library of Congress Cataloging in Publication Data

McClure, Vimala Schneider, 1952—
    The tao of motherhood / by Vimala McClure.
        p. cm.
    Adaptation of: Tao te ching.
    Includes bibliographical references.
    ISBN 0-945934-05-X : $10.95
    1. Parenting—Religious aspects—Taoism. 2.
Lao-tzu. Tao te ching. I. Lao-tzu. Tao te ching.
II. Title.
BL1900.L36M33 1991
299'.5144—dc20

                                    91-14290
                                            CIP

Printed in the United States of America

Table of Contents

Preface

Twenty years ago, on a summer's evening, I slipped into a chair on a big porch in Denver, Colorado and listened to Vimala sing. I sat behind her, hoping that my presence would not disturb the sweet music and devotional sentiment that brought tears to my eyes. Today as I read *The Tao of Motherhood* new tears came, and reminded me of those tears years ago.

Those first years in Denver that I knew Vimala, we both worked in a large house filled with young people trying to guide a spiritual and social service organization. I remember Vimala as a quiet but powerful soul who seemed to stay out of the battles, but always got what she needed. Someone who sat back and watched what went on and then made the precise move needed to reestablish balance.

When Vimala does take action, she pours herself into it, leaving a clear path behind her for those who might follow. When she had to give birth by Caesarean section and felt unprepared for the experience, she helped form the Caesarian Birth Education Group in Boulder, Colorado in 1977. After seeing infant massage when she worked in an orphanage in India, she tried it out, very successfully, with her colicky son. She began teaching other parents, and by the time her second baby was born, she was teaching others to be instructors. From those small beginnings has grown The International Association of Infant Massage Instructors, which now has instructors teaching parents to massage their babies in 15 countries.

When Vimala sees a need, she looks for practical ways that she can make a difference. While others may talk or complain, Vimala takes action. When her spiritual teacher was being mistreated in prison, she compiled the evidence and wrote a book to spread the information. She wanted to learn Bengali, so she put together a superlearning program to help others, and became a proficient

speaker in the process. When she fell in love with Bangladesh, she wrote a book for children, called *Bangladesh: Rivers in a Crowded Land*. To help women apply spirituality to their lives, she produced *Some Still Want the Moon, A Woman's Introduction to Tantra Yoga*.

The Tao of Motherhood has grown out of a period in Vimala's life when she has seen her children grow both closer to her and further away. She has watched them become teenagers, struggle with family changes, and make decisions which stretched her as their mother. She has formed a new family from two, watching the years it took for balance to again settle in.

As with all true artists, both pain and joy have contributed to her work. Vimala has struggled with poverty, health problems and abuse at different times in her life. But she has taken them and mixed them with deep thought, love, and spiritual bliss, and come up with the inspiration and discipline to manifest practical works. Works such as the *Tao of Motherhood*, which, though based on an ancient text, helps us parent in a very modern, very stressful world.

One last story to share. I attended a training of infant massage instructors that Vimala was leading in 1984. One father in the demonstration class was particularly rough with his baby, just simply because he was a big and tough, but loving person. When a concerned trainee asked if we shouldn't be trying to temper his enthusiasm in order to protect the baby, Vimala pointed out, "Remember that every child and every parent has a completely unique and special relationship. That child knows his dad and loves his dad. Our job is to watch that communication, to nurture it, and to support the parents in their heart-to-heart relationships with their children." I see that idea, too, in *The Tao of Motherhood*.

You and your child have a unique and very special relationship.

The dos and don'ts of all the advice givers out there may or may not apply to you. You have to listen to your heart and to your child and then make the decisions that are good for right now, for you two.

A lot of water has flowed under the bridge in the twenty years I have known Vimala. I now have four children, and she has three. Like other mothers and women everywhere throughout time, we reach out to each other to share our joys and fears, our spirituality, our reality and yes, our tears.

May your parenting be fulfilling and satisfying for both you and your little ones.

Jody Wright

Jody Wright is the mother of four daughters, a founding member of the International Association of Infant Massage Instructors, a La Leche League Leader, and with her husband, Prakash Laufer, the owner of Motherwear, a catalog designed for nursing mothers.

Introduction

Since before the birth of my first child, parenting has been an important and integral part of my spiritual path. Having meditated daily for several years before my first pregnancy, I wanted to continue my practice. But I knew that pregnancy and young children added a level of chaos into life which seemed to be in conflict with the stillness and quiet—the solitude—of meditation. My search for a way to continue functioning as a spiritual seeker led to much thinking about spirituality and its place in everyday life.

When my first child was born it was time for me to begin practicing in earnest a lesson which was part of my instruction in meditation. The lesson is called *madhuvidya* in Sanskrit ("sweet knowledge"), and it is the act of infusing spirituality into every aspect of life. It is the conscious process of perceiving the unity of all things, of trying to understand deep within oneself that everything is sacred. Infant Massage was a wonderful tool, and became an important part of my relationship with my children. I shared this with other parents in my book *Infant Massage: a Handbook for Loving Parents.*

As my children grew our relationships provided so much growth for me. In order to give them what they needed—respect, acceptance, encouragement, boundaries, assistance, understanding, and above all unconditional love—I had to learn about these things for myself. Everything I had learned about spirituality was tested. Children are mirrors; they will always show you exactly what is going on inside of you. Each phase of their growth is an opportunity to heal your own pain, to go deeper inside yourself and become more truly human.

Parenting is a spiritual path which can bring you great pain and great joy and which can have a tremendous positive impact on your personality and behavior. I believe our children, unknowingly and with innocent trickery, teach us the deeper knowledge of how to be a true human being.

My heart has learned its lessons from meditation and mothering. This book has given me a chance to distill some of those lessons through the vehicle of the wonderful Taoist teachings of Lao Tzu.

I hope you find inspiration here, and that your journey with your child is a joyful one which teaches you what you came here to learn.

Dedicated to my mother

*T*ao is the oneness of all things.

You and your child come from One and journey toward One. You are essentially the same.

Right mothering springs from this knowledge: the One in either responds to the One in both. The bond is oneness, and cannot be broken.

When doubt and uncertainty arise, return to this simple truth. Be in oneness and the illusion of separateness dies.

Be still and allow unity to be revealed.

Like the eternal Tao, a wise mother gives birth but does not possess. She meets the child's needs yet requires no gratitude.

Observe how great masters raise up their dearest disciples. Observe how nature raises up the plants and animals.

Great teachers take no credit for their students' growth, yet they will go to any length to teach them what they need to know. Nature requires no praise, yet it provides for the needs of earth's inhabitants.

Mother is the reflective principle, the balancing agent for the child. Like a guru, she allows the child to make mistakes and loves the child without condition. Like nature, she allows consequences to unfold and balance to be restored when it is lost.

She intervenes only when the right use of power is required.

*R*ight mothering meets the child's need.

Focusing on what the child should *not* be draws resistant energy. Pointing out what the child *should* be feeds self-hatred and struggle.

Ask yourself, "What is my child telling me about his needs at this moment?" This is not always easy. One child's needs may be more obvious—or more acceptable—than another's.

Meeting needs and obeying commands are not the same. The wise obey the Divine Law and thus fulfill the need of the moment through action or non-action. They are responsive, not tyrannized.

This has nothing to do with what society says is proper. It has everything to do with the Infinite Good as it flows through the here and now.

Do not reward performance. Rather, respond to Spirit expressing the Way. You are a mirror with which your child sees—and corrects—himself.

Remember, you and your child are travelers through infinite time. How you interact is important enough to change lifetimes of karma; yet it is an insignificant drop in the ocean of relationship through which you both move.

Keep in mind the endless nature of being, and your journey will gain perspective.

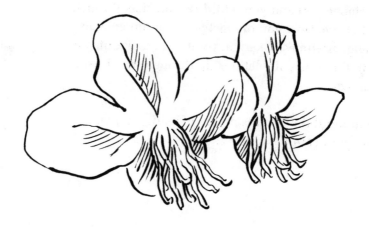

$\mathcal{R}$aise up your children with great reverence for the Consciousness that moves in them. Treat them with respect, even in their infancy, for they are not yours.

Reverence and respect are not the same as worship; children thrive on benevolent neglect.

The child who feels your respect during silences is nourished more than the child who is constantly fussed and chattered over.

Mother is the feminine principle. She represents the yin, the anima, the receptive, the earth. Though she must at times take the role of the masculine principle, it is the feminine which gives her power and from which she draws her strength.

She teaches her daughters to respect their feminine nature. She teaches her sons to respect their feminine side and thus all women.

The truly feminine mother never cringes or defers. Her strength is unshakable, like the earth upon which we walk but which can topple us with a single deep breath.

*E*verything which endures can only do so because Eternal Consciousness gives it sentience.

A mother who gives herself completely to her infant meets herself in the dark and finds fulfillment.

In the hours between midnight and dawn, she crosses the threshold of self-concern and discovers a Self that has no limits. A wise mother meets this Presence with humility and steps through time into selflessness.

Infants know when their mothers have done this, and they become peaceful.

Who, then, is the doer? Is it the infant who brings its mother through the veil of self-concern into limitlessness? Is it the mother, who chooses to hold sacred her infant's needs and surrender herself? Or is it the One, which weaves them both through a spiraling path toward wholeness?

You can sit and meditate while your baby cries himself to sleep. Or you can go to him and share his tears, and find your Self.

*W*ater benefits us without taking from us. It cleanses us, nourishes us, and calms our restlessness.

So is a mother to her child. From the moment of birth, a child's well-being is her only concern.

A wise mother cleans and discards the child's waste without comment. The child's excrement, its tears, its rages, are all allowed to be and discarded without emotion.

A wise mother does not judge her child.

There is great power in being a mother. It is easy to think you control your child and his destiny; that you can mold him into your ideal; that his imperfections are yours to correct.

The power of a mother's love is like gold in a temple. Used for personal aggrandizement it brings pain and suffering. Hoarded, it benefits no one. Used rightly, with benevolence, in time of great need, it serves.

When you are about to use your power in your relationship with your child, think again. Is there another way to accomplish your goal?

Retreat and be still. Contemplate your choices. When you choose to use your power, use it justly, with great calm, and do not waiver.

*S*trive for clarity in your own life. What motivates
your feelings? We often live out the past over and
over in our relationships. We sometimes fail to see the
real child, for we have superimposed our own pain
upon our children.

Clear yourself. Find the Child within you, heal her,
and set her free. As long as the child in you weeps
and cringes, your power as a mother will remain
confused.

Polish the mirror of the self and your child will see
herself more clearly.

The empty spaces make wholeness. The emptiness in a pot makes it valuable; you can fill it with food or water.

Pay attention to what isn't. Listen for what your child does not say. Observe what she does not do.

Similarly, know that your child uses your empty spaces. What you do not say resounds. What you do not do impresses.

*L*ife with children is naturally noisy. Can you find
the silence within the noise? Can you feel the peace
within the turmoil?

If you cannot reflect in the chaos of the moment,
withdraw. Make time for yourself to turn inward and
digest your life.

Whether you realize it or not, Mother is the pivot of
the family. Not you, but the eternal Mother
expressing Itself through your choices.

To allow the Mother principle to work to center your
family, take time for yourself. Otherwise, the self will
be constantly grasping for its share. This grasping
obscures the Mother principle from within you and
from your family, and leaves everyone alone and lost.

It is said, "She who values her body more than dominion over the empire can be given custody of the empire." Taking care of yourself is your right and your responsibility.

If a mother values herself, her children value her. She teaches self-esteem by her example. Her peaceful demeanor communicates love to all who come in contact with her.

Knowing when to sacrifice the self and when to nurture the self comes with daily mindfulness. Pay attention to your body's signals. Observing your feelings each day, eventually you will be able to take time for yourself before it becomes an angry demand. This enables you to give of yourself appropriately, without resentment.

$\mathcal{P}$arenting is at times confusing. There will be moments when you truly do not know. Should you exert your authority or step back? Should you give advice or remain silent? Should you offer help or allow a mistake to be made?

When you cannot see what is happening, relax and look gently with your inner eye. The harder you try to take hold of a situation, the more difficult it becomes.

Let go. Trust in the Way which follows its own flow. Allow the Great to live in you and work through you for your child's greater good.

Return to the core: a relationship of love is more worthwhile than a philosophical position. When doubt arises, give way only to love.

The ancient teachers demonstrated their realization of the Way. These ancient teachers were often women. They were mothers and sisters, aunts and grandmothers. They meditated. Through their relationships, they taught the art of being.

Because they meditated, their depth made them seem inscrutable and their wisdom profound. The truth is, they simply knew how to be human.

They observed behaviors and acted with precision and care, never acting recklessly. They behaved with dignity and grace and won the respect of others without trying. They respected others and treated children as human beings.

They were strong yet yielding, like ice ready to melt. They were simple, like the uncarved block of wood. They were receptive like a valley between high mountains. They were full of life and involved in their families, yet they were able to be still and become as deep and clear as pure water.

These ancient grandmothers did not need to go away into the caves or forests to become enlightened. They were enlightenment itself.

*E*verything arises from Consciousness and returns.

The universe is the play of the rising and returning of millions of beings, all becoming One. You and your child are both on this path too.

It is impossible to keep this awareness of your destiny awakened all the time. But daily meditation can bring awareness to your thoughts and actions.

Awareness brings constancy to your relationships. Constancy allows your child to release fear and follow his destiny.

Meditate on Oneness. Release the small self to the Infinite, and the Infinite will take care of Itself.

A wise mother does not unnecessarily interfere with her child's life.

Your children have their own process—their own thoughts, feelings, and reactions—which must be allowed to unfold.

If your childhood was painful you may get overinvolved with your children's lives and smother them. Or you may find yourself forcing them to think and feel the way you do, to adopt all your values and live the life you wish you had.

If you do not trust your children's process, your children cannot trust anyone or anything. Your confidence in them builds their confidence in themselves.

Assist your children in such a way that they think, "We did it ourselves!"

*W*hen you forget that you and your children are instruments of the One, dogma takes over.

You begin to think in judgments of yourself and others:

"All mothers should (*stay home, have a career, be involved with school, help with homework, keep a spotless home…*), therefore I'm not a good mother if I don't."

Or; "All children should (*be polite, respect their elders, help at home, get good grades, win in sports, be popular, appreciate good music, read great books…*), therefore my children are bad if they don't."

When truth is forgotten, acceptance, tolerance, compassion and flexibility give way to judgmentalism, intolerance, meanness and rigidity. Hypocrisy follows.

Children who are closer to their birth and thus to the experience of Oneness, rightly reject hypocrisy.

Throw away gadgets. Discard expert opinions. Forget the toys to stimulate intelligence. Don't buy devices to simulate what is real.

Return to the real. Connect with your children heart-to-heart. Let them gaze at you, at trees and water and sky. Let them feel their pain. Feel it with them.

Touch them with your hands, your eyes and your heart. Let them bond with the living, breathing world. Let them feel their feelings and teach them their names.

Return to the uncarved simplicity.

The real education teaches us to be whole human beings.

Be concerned with this: that you, your marriage, and your home teach health and balance and truth.

Any further education merely augments this basic course.

The wise remain aware of the spirituality of life.

Every mother has felt the stillness and the stir of
Eternal Consciousness in her womb. Remember that.

Bring that mysterious, silent moment into the
clamoring present.

*T*ruth is in paradox:

Surrender and you get everything. Bend and be strong.

When you reach your limit and are exhausted, new energy rises in you. When you release others, they come to you. The wise know this: Let go in order to preserve.

Be empty and fulfilled.

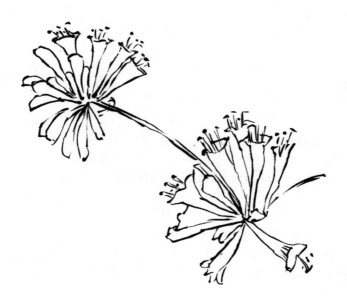

There is no natural pouring-forth that lasts forever. When it rains, it stops. The wind blows, and then it ceases.

Learn to use your words wisely, to communicate rather than to lecture. Speak your truth, state your feelings, then stop. Your actions, in silence, speak louder and will be heard.

Teach your children this: A human being is greater than a human doing.

*Y*our children are not you.

To try to show the world what a good mother you are diminishes you. To try to show the world what good children you have diminishes them.

Heal your insecurity by holding to the truth. The One Consciousness flows through all without boasting.

Eternal Consciousness is not a thing. It has many
names and no name. It is within and beyond
everything. It is the essence of us all.

Your child depends on you. You depend on the
earth. The earth depends on the universe. The
universe depends on the Supreme.

The Supreme is subject to nothing. It is the Great
Mother, and She holds you in the palm of her hand.

*P*ay attention and stay centered.

You carry the mantle of "Mother," the eternal principle of balance and stability.

When your children's energy is scattered, be grounded. When your children throw tantrums, be still. Know what you stand for.

Be firm and consistent to teach your children about boundaries. Thus you will root them in health and release their souls to limitlessness.

Someone who travels often knows the best routes.
Someone who speaks for a living knows when to
pause. Someone who works with numbers knows
how to add and subtract in her head.

A wise mother knows: It is her state of consciousness
that matters.

Her gentleness and clarity command respect. Her love
creates security.

To learn the Way, children need to respect the Mother.
To learn the Way, mothers need to cherish the Child.

Thus each follows nature and finds the Self.

A mother must know how to assert her warrior side, how to wield power and make decisions, how to inspire discipline and set boundaries. But she must hold to the feminine to be truly effective.

The most powerful mothers are healers. Their surgeon's knives cut but do not sever. They nourish and listen.

A wise mother knows the One Consciousness works through her.

*A*void pushing too hard. Your children are full of
spirit and will find their way. Their true parent
resides within them; you are only a reflection.

Mothers who constantly interfere—who push and
challenge, who lecture and berate—think they are
molding their children into good citizens. In fact,
they are destroying confidence and inviting scorn.

Know when to intervene and how. Do it with
gentleness, firmness, swiftness and respect.
And then release the child to the Way.

*Y*our children will challenge you and your power.
Do not use force or intimidation to manage them.

Remember, wars bring suffering to all. The winners
and the losers both have bitter harvests.

When your child engages you in conflict, bring it full
circle without physical, mental or emotional violence.

Withdraw, be still. Try to understand what the child
needs, whether it be a firm boundary or a listening
heart. Then calmly exert your authority with love to
end the conflict and restore harmony.

When you feel angry with your child, know that
something rational must be done. State your feelings
honestly, then withdraw to process your emotions
and make a plan.

Striking out, either physically or emotionally, may
succeed in getting through to the child, but it will also
plant the seeds of guilt. Guilt is followed by
resentment and bitterness. A victory can therefore
end in failure.

Too many such victories and you will witness the
death of your child's trust.

The Way cannot be defined; it is only when you are in its flow that it becomes known to you.

If parents, the guardians of the human race, could hold to the Way, children would naturally grow strong and healthy in body, mind and spirit. Nothing special would be needed.

Because we have forgotten the Way, roadmaps and instructions have come into being.

One must know when to put aside the instructions and find the Way.

The single most important instruction is this: Meditate on the Eternal. As the river finds the sea, you will find the Way.

Contentment *33*

*Y*ou can know your children with some intelligence.
Knowing yourself requires enlightenment.

You can manage your children with strength.
Mastering your own life requires true power.

To accept what you are is to be content, and
contentment is the greatest wealth. To work with
patience is to gather power. To surrender to the
Eternal flow is to be completely present.

Eternal Consciousness is everywhere, in everything. Everything depends on it and it guides all things.

Though it is the source of every atom of the universe, nothing can affect it. No one can own it. It lives in every blade of grass and every human being, without discrimination.

A wise mother is like the Eternal One. She shines in her children's eyes.

If you hold to the Eternal in thought, word and action,
your children will return again and again to you.

Your children may not understand the depth of your
parenting until later. They may question your values
and say you are "weird" or not like other kids' parents.

They may say your life is boring or strange.
Nevermind. The wise are not caught up in appearances.

The Way is at times boring in its simplicity. Hold to it.
The superficial eventually repels.

That which is real attracts every good thing to it.

If you want to know what to do, learn to look at things upside down. To receive, you must give. Those who boast are insecure. Silence speaks louder than words. The strongest warrior never shows his sword. The soft overcomes the hard.

Here is an exercise: When you feel a hardness come around your heart, go soft and explore the sensations and feelings that arise. Feel what is beneath anger: thousands of tiny moments of pain, confusion, doubt, fear, self-protection. Accept all this as part of you. Look on yourself with kindness.

Now notice the quality of your heart. How different it is from the hard edge of control that springs from fear.

A wise parent does little, yet so much gets done!

After all, the Eternal does nothing, yet the entire universe goes on.

When you get too busy, stop and return to center. When you are centered, you easily keep things in order. When things are in order, there is not much to do.

A wise parent does little, yet so much gets done!

If you leave parenting to the unconscious process, you will blindly repeat unhealthy parenting you may have received.

If your childhood was not happy and secure, you may try too hard to be an ideal parent.

There are choices to be made every day. Reject the rigid and favor the firm. Reject criticism and favor support. Reject permissiveness and favor negotiation. Reject abandonment and favor direction.

Choose the fruit, not the flower.
Choose the berry, not the chaff.
Choose the inner, not the outer.

Conscious choice is the hallmark of healthy parenting.

There is a natural order of things: the seasons change,
the tides well up and recede, the moon circles and
women's bodies respond.

The sky is clear.
The earth is solid.
The unseen forces are powerful.
The valley is full of life.
Every atom dances with Consciousness.

Look around: Everything follows its nature;
wholeness results.

Imagine what would happen if nature did not follow
its biological programming.

The sky would shatter.
The earth would explode.
The unseen forces would run amok.
The valley would go barren.
Everything would lose Consciousness and die
into the void.

Oneness is the root of balance. When you can follow
your own nature in balance, you will provide exactly
what your children need.

We all come from the One and return to it.

Stop and bring your consciousness into this moment.
Let your heart absorb your mind. Can you feel the
oneness that connects you with your child?

Surrendering to the One is the Way.

Everything comes from Being. Being springs from that
which is beyond Being.

A wise mother learns each day from quiet listening.
Her parenting springs from her children's changing
needs.

An average mother hears the lessons but wonders how
to be, and forgets what she learns. She is often filled
with guilt and is indecisive and irritable.

A foolish mother dismisses what her soul hears in
favor of what the experts tell her. She is rigid and
controlling, boastful and full of fear.

The best parenting springs from simple love.
The wise attune themselves to a child's true need
and steadfastly follow it. Thus, they cannot be called
"permissive" or "harsh."

What is right for each child may not be right for all
children. What is right cannot always be proven in a
laboratory.

The One is born from beyond One. One becomes
two, and two becomes three.

That which is beyond consciousness gives birth to
consciousness, which gives birth to mind, which gives
birth to matter and all the ten thousand things. The
ten thousand things maintain a balance between
centrifugal and centripetal forces.

The ten thousand things hold Eternal Consciousness
within them and thus are magnetized back to the One.

Things harmonize opposites and seek the One.

You must be a child to be a parent. The infant is
parent to its mother.

To move in balance toward One, make sure you learn
more from your child than you teach her.

Soft overcomes hard. Who you are means more to your child than what you teach.

When your heart is hard and the bitter taste of strong words is in your mouth, step back.

Let mind go into soft heart. Breathe kindness and remain quiet.

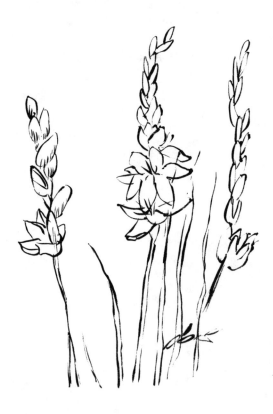

*W*hich is dearer to you: being right or being respected?

Being respected or being loved?

Having or being?

Know when to let your child go, to have her own life and feelings. Your security is within you, not within your child.

Grasp and you will lose. Release and find contentment.

The best mothering looks like no mothering.

Smothering heats up, stillness cools. Be a still, cool stream for your child's agitation.

A serene mother rocks the universe in her arms and all is well.

When your life is in order, your child finds balance.

When you cease to listen with your heart, war breaks out. When you lose sight of the big picture, you fight and quarrel over trifles and no one wins.

There is no greater pain than feeling you are not enough.

Your child is enough, right now, just the way he is. And so are you.

All you need to know is within you.

Your child's spirit teaches you how to guide her.

Be present. What is happening right now? Be still
and comprehend with your inner senses. Talk to the
inner child, setting aside theories.

If your child was taken from you tomorrow, would
this matter today?

*F*irst time mothers read all the books and cling to theories and gadgets.

Fifth time mothers have taken it all in and let it sink into the unconscious. Equipment has worn out and the child is given wooden spoons and the easy company of present-focused people.

The youngest child is usually the most relaxed!

*B*e open to your child's individual needs and expression. One child needs stimulation, the next needs quiet. One needs to be carried all the time, another likes to play nearby with the freedom to extend his limbs.

A wise mother knows: there is no good child and no bad child. There is only *this* child.

When you have your first child, suddenly life
becomes precious. So precious you can strangle it
with the tension of holding on.

What mother hasn't had fearful fantasies of losing her
child? This is the hardest time to accept letting go as
part of holding on.

Three mothers in ten grasp their children with claws
of steel to protect them from harm.

Three mothers in ten allow their children to wander
into danger.

Three mothers in ten confuse their children with
endless admonitions and worries, yet force them to
face pain before they are ready.

Only ten percent accept the wheel of life as it is.
They are free from fear, for they know that nothing
is ever lost. They do not grasp and cling or organize
their lives around a fantasy of what might happen.

For their children, fear cannot find a place to lodge its
blade.

*E*verything comes from One consciousness. The
harmonious rhythms we call happiness. The
discordant rhythms we call pain.

Your child is attracted to the One in you, to the Way
which nurtures, shelters, guides and protects. It flows
from you, harmonious with the world from which
your child has come.

The Supreme nurtures without grasping, shelters
without claiming, guides without interfering and
protects without smothering.

The closer you are to the Way, the more your child
will trust you.

The Mother of all is that from which you draw your mothering. It is the eternal balance, the breathing, beating womb from which all creation arises. It is eternally giving birth, eternally conceiving.

Close your mouth and allow the Mother of all to speak in you.

Keep busy, fluttering and chattering, and you cannot hear Her voice.

Observe the child to know the mother.

Observe the insignificant to know what matters.

$\mathcal{A}$ wise mother keeps her child's life simple. She gives away ten thousand toys and keeps only that which is useful.

She lets her baby gaze into her face and at the wondrous colors of nature.

She gives her child household things and tells stories the same way over and over.

Feeling that you must have every toy, every device, every piece of equipment merely places objects between you and your child. You have to work that much harder to provide them; work which robs your child of his most important stimulation—your company.

Those who become trapped in the cycle of getting and having spend their children's lives in a kind of fog. The best moments are lost forever.

Ask the question: Who really benefits from all this consumption?

*R*ight mothering is honored from generation to generation. Like an old tree with untold roots, it holds firm through countless storms.

Behave toward yourself with loving kindness, and serenity will emanate from you.

When you are serene, your life is in order.

When your life is in order, your family is harmonious.

Your family affects your community. Your community influences your culture. Your culture influences the world.

How do I know? Just by looking around.

The energy that comes from the Infinite moves
through you and enlightens your being.

When you have released your fear and found your
Self, you can be in harmony with your child because
you are attuned to the same energy.

In this space you are relaxed and soft, bendable.
Things don't bother you, energy flows. You can walk
the baby all night long; her cries do not challenge you.

Your power is in place without exerting it.

$\mathcal{A}$ wise parent knows her intuition is the only authority worth listening to. She understands its function and filters advice through it.

Rigid styles characterize the insecure parent who needs to protect her own inner child with fear. She is full of "don'ts."

A wise parent refrains from too much talk. Her inner calm brings peace to troubled hearts and resolution to conflicts. She doesn't need anyone's approval but her own.

At each stage of your child's life she needs
demonstrations of your love and your support.

Your love comforts and accepts. It is a mirror in
which your child sees herself as beautiful and worthy.

Your support encourages and affirms; it is a
springboard toward independence.

Too many rules turn facilitation into interference,
affection into business. Let your child help set her
own limits against which she can push now and then.

Be firm without being rigid. You child will grow up
with lots of healthy personal power.

*H*ealthy parenting can be a challenge if your own childhood wasn't healthy. It requires energy, attention, and constant restraint. These all come naturally from healthy parent-child bonds.

If the parenting you received was rigid, abandoning, or inconsistent, you may find yourself exhausted by your children. Realize that you need healing. Take time out to nurture yourself.

You can make the choice to be a healthy parent. You can learn how to trust what is happening and behave appropriately. You can find a healthy model and follow it.

Unhealthy parenting disables with wounds that are hard to heal. Right mothering is a potent healer, readily available to the natural wounds of life.

In bringing up children there is nothing like restraint. This requires deep roots in your own spirituality, because it means releasing your own ideas in favor of perceiving each child's needs.

Prayer, meditation and the like can help you stay centered and aware of the deeper levels of what is happening. Take the time you need for your spiritual growth.

Cultivate limitlessness, and you will know how and when to set limits for your children.

As much as possible, let your children find their own way. Mother them delicately, like frying eggplant.

Negative states will arise, express, and pass away. Allow this to happen. Help the child to become aware of this process gently, without intrusion. The wise parent does not fight fire with fire.

Be a mirror. Let your child see how cause and effect works in life. Too much interference and advice gives power to opposing forces.

The mother's energy is so powerful because of her feminine receptivity. She yields and conquers through her calm.

The child's energy dominates. He feels so powerful! Only the mother knows it is her strength upon which he draws to build himself.

Thus both reach their goal of independence.

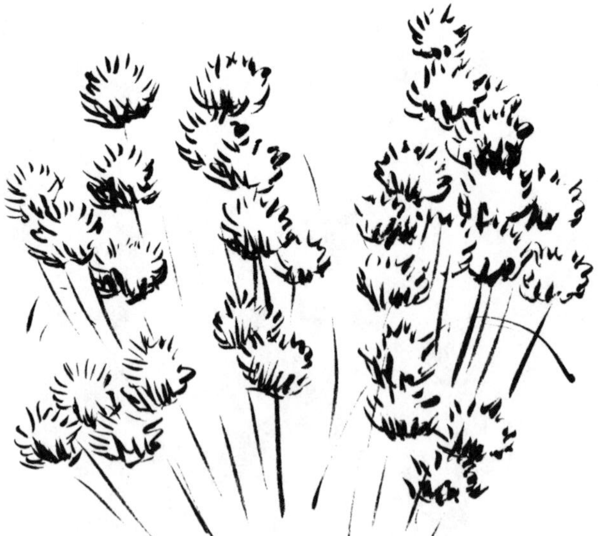

*K*nowing how things work is helpful to you. But remember, mothers have mothered since the dawn of time, and it all seems to work out in the end.

If you don't know your intuition, it is no crime. However, if you know how things work, you are fortunate. Your behavior will be more effective, your words will have more power, your decisions will be good ones.

Since ancient times people have revered those whose spiritual faculties are well developed.

If you want to help your children build themselves, you must act without seeming to act. Through gestures, small words, and most of all through your own example, your children will gradually grow wings.

Your baby is learning to trust you. Touch and hold her and smile into her eyes. Allow her to feel all her feelings.

Your toddler is learning to trust the earth. Support and protect him. Allow him to explore.

Your preschooler is learning to trust herself. Help her learn appropriate choices. Allow her to say no and test her limits.

Your young child is learning to trust relationships with others. Affirm his ability to learn how to express his feelings and ask for help. Allow him to ask questions.

Your older child is learning to trust society. Provide accurate information, offer problem-solving tools, and encourage responsibility. Allow her to experience consequences while remaining safe in your love and support.

Your adolescent is learning to trust himself as an adult. Celebrate his growing up. Talk about your own feelings at his age. Allow him to explore choices that may be different from yours.

Know your child's needs at each stage and anticipate her struggles. In this way you can offer assistance without seeming to assist.

*L*ove your children while they are small. Spend time with them now. Don't put it off for a single moment.

The rigid tree begins as a pliant sapling. A huge building begins as a shovelful of dirt. A thousand mile journey begins under your feet.

Everything depends on early influences. You can't go back later and bond with your children in the same way.

Many parents get anxious with their teenagers and try to make up for lost time. When the child needs wings, they try to root him and spoil everything.

Conscious mothering requires careful choices, from beginning to end.

The ancient mothers knew. There was no need for books and experts.

Today we have lost much. We need to re-learn the Way.

Be cautious about what the experts tell you. What sounds complex and clever may have no roots. Wisdom has no cleverness in it. It is pure and simple, and when it is practiced the results are obvious.

The wise assist a child's being rather than his doing.

The sea is the greatest of all the waters because it allows the rivers and streams to empty into it.

Parents with the greatest power in their children's lives are those to which the child can go without fear.

The wise mother facilitates her child's growth with firm, loving kindness. She receives his mistakes and tantrums with equanimity.

Because she does not push, harass or manipulate, she does not invite rebellion. Her children love and respect her and trust her with their pain.

*E*veryone says the Eternal One is great. Because it is great it is beyond our comprehension. If we could hold it in our minds, it would be limited. If it is limited, it is not the Way.

There are three treasures which are invaluable to you as a parent:

The first is kindness.
The second is simplicity.
The third is humility.

If you are kind, you can act with courage to support and protect your children.

If you keep your life simple, you have lots of time to give them.

If you know yourself as a human being—no more, no less—you teach your children without imposing on them.

A parent who is protective without being kind, whose life is busy and complicated, who demands respect and expects perfection, loses her children in the end.

Loving kindness, simplicity, and humility are the treasures your children will inherit.

A good soldier is never hateful. A good fighter is not angry. A good employer encourages leadership.

The best parenting shows choices rather than delivering ultimatums.

Empowerment is the natural means to grow a good human being.

*W*hen your children push against their limits and your boundaries, consider the advice of the ancient strategists: do not allow yourself to be baited into fighting fire with fire. Keep your center. Calmly and clearly show them their choices.

This is winning the battle without showing your sword.

If you try to overpower your children you will discover a simple truth: their power is greater than yours! Thus you surrender your treasure and respect is lost.

In a battle of wills, loving kindness is the only weapon that conquers.

Bringing up children in this way is easy to understand and easy to do. But not many parents are able to follow it.

The Way is ancient and follows truth. It is known to those who are truly human. But parents today have lost their roots and rely on the latest gimmicks and the opinions of medical technicians.

The wise are known only by a few. Their wisdom is concealed. The wise mother's precious gem is hidden in the pocket of her apron.

*A*dmit you don't know everything. Admit you may not know anything.

To pretend that you know when you don't leads to pain. When you are tired of pain, you will no longer create it. This is the secret of good health.

Children who grow up with no spirituality—with no sense of wonder—will struggle with depression as adults.

Do not impose rational thinking on your children too early. Do not oppress them with adult reality.

Because you don't pressure them to grow up, they can grow naturally and keep their sweetness.

The wise parent can be childlike but is not irresponsible, loves herself but is not selfish. She is spiritual but not dogmatic.

There are two kinds of courage.

There is the passionate bravery which gets people killed. This kind of courage is inherent; either you have it or you don't. It is the bravery of a mother who would die shielding her child from a killer's bullet.

The second type of courage is developed through daily practice. It is the inner strength to do what must be done, to make rational plans and carry them out, to face difficulty and overcome obstacles. It is the bravery of a mother who makes personal sacrifices for her children's well-being, and then is able to let them go to their own destinies.

*M*any parents discover too late that one cannot raise children well with punishment as the core of discipline. Hit your child and eventually the child's rage will be greater than your censure.

Prisons are filled with "well-disciplined" people.

A good parent helps a child to learn how his behavior affects his own life through natural consequences. This is how true inner discipline is cultivated.

A master carpenter cuts cleanly and quickly and makes furniture which endures. When you deliver harsh, judgmental consequences, you are trying to do nature's job. Like an inexperienced carpenter, you are bound to make a mess of it and only hurt yourself.

Children starve if their parents eat all the food.

Children rebel if their parents brook no compromise.

Children have no love for life if their parents squeeze
it out of them. They spend their lives grieving for
their lost joy.

Begin to notice when you are critical and controlling
with your child. Observe yourself and check your behavior
before it gets acted out.

Find out what you need and give it to yourself.
When the little child in you gets the love, support and
encouragement it needs, your critical behavior will
naturally disappear.

*H*uman bodies are gentle and flexible when living but hard and stiff when dead.

Living plants are tender and green when living but dry and brittle when dead.

To be hard and unbending is to be dead. Without flexibility, there is no juice. What is the point of living then?

*W*hen people are in harmony with spiritual laws,
everything is in balance. The excess is reduced, the
deficient is expanded, everyone's needs are met and
life is full of joy.

When we lose the Way, we lose our balance and life is
full of pain. We take from those who do not have
enough and give to those who have too much.

A mother who walks in balance has more than
enough. She enters her children's lives and surrounds
them with love when their heart-reserves are low.
She allows them to do the same for her.

She understands the cyclic nature of things, the way
the bow contracts and expands to receive and release
the arrow.

Paradox

There is nothing more receptive and flowing than water, yet there is nothing better for polishing stone.

A mother's nature is paradox. Your strength is in gentleness. Your authority is in receptivity. Your power is in letting go.

As your children grow up, there is bound to be some unresolved pain. There was the time you couldn't make it to the third grade play. The time you struck your child in anger. The painful divorce which could not be adequately explained.

A wise parent recognizes her failings and accepts what is. There is room in life for remorse, and for forgiveness. There is room in our hearts for ourselves, and for one another.

*K*eep your life simple and serenity will follow.

Like a small country with little need for supersonic travel, a simple life has little need for tension and stress.

Give your children yourself and the need for things is minimal.

*T*ell the truth,

Say what is happening.

Allow what is, and allow it to be known.

Bring your children up in a home which is clean and clear and honest. There is no greater legacy you can give them.

Bibliography

English, Jane and Gia-Fu Feng, translators. Lao Tsu. *Tao Te Ching.* New York: Vintage Books, 1772

Heider, John. *The Tao of Leadership.* Atlanta: Humanics New Age, 1985.

Iyer, Raghavan, Ed. Lao Tzu. *Tao Te Ching: The Book of Perfectibility.* London: Concord Grove Press, 1983.

Lau, D. C., translator. Lao Tzu. *Tao Te Ching.* London: Penguin Books, 1963.

Waley, Arthur. *The Way and Its Power.* New York: Grove Press, 1958.

Wu, John C.H., translator. Lao Tzu. *Tao Teh Ching.* Boston: Shambhala, 1989.

About the Author

Vimala McClure lives and writes in the Ozarks of Southern Missouri. She is the author of the classic *Infant Massage, A Handbook for Loving Parents* and founder of the International Association of Infant Massage Instructors. She has been practicing and teaching meditation in the Tantric tradition for 22 years, and wrote *Some Still Want the Moon: a Woman's Introduction to Tantra Yoga, The Ethics of Love: Using Yoga's Timeless Wisdom to Heal Yourself, Your Family & the Earth* and a book for children: *Bangladesh: Rivers in a Crowded Land.*

Vimala is also a textile artist. Her quilts have won awards in regional and national shows, have been featured in national magazines, and are exhibited in galleries and private collections.

Vimala has three teenage children.